From Managing Strippers to Managing Truckers:
Same Grind, Different Hustle

Courtney C Petty

- © 2018 Courtney C Petty

All rights reserved

Library of Congress Cataloging-in-Publication Data has been applied for

Petty, Courtney C
From Managing Strippers to Managing Truckers: Same Grind, Different Hustle

ISBN: 978-1-732-5968-1-8

Contents

Introduction 4
1 High School 6
2 Life or Death: Preeclampsia – Eclampsia 26
3 Life After High School 35
4 The Central Station 46
5 Lollipop Entertainment 55
6 Clay Co. 61
7 An Unexpected Tragedy 65
8 Bumble Bee 71
9 The Trucking Business 76
10 Reflection and Vision 80
Contact / Booking/ Get Involved 83

Introduction

I would first like to thank you for purchasing my book. I am so ecstatic that I am able to tell readers about my journey from managing dancers to managing truckers.

I am 32 years old and I make over six figures a year, mainly working from home. I am financially stable and independent with two kids. I hope my story will encourage you to keep striving and never give up.

Everyone that knows me well would say that I've always been a hustler. When it came to business, I was never scared to try any and everything to one day make it in life.

My mother was an entrepreneur ever since I was little. She had a cleaning business in which she was her own boss, so I guess you could say that I have that same entrepreneurial spirit. I started working when I was 15 while in high school and I would purchase my own school clothes and shoes. And, I was always getting my hair and nails done without my parents having to pay for it. I was independent, I guess, for a 15-year-old. Back then, I would love going to work so I could buy things for myself; it felt good having my own money. I didn't really save much nor did I have anyone teaching me anything about saving. Nowadays, I'm all about saving, investing and making my money work for me by obtaining assets, for one.

I will say that life will teach you lessons and the lessons that I have learned taught me so much about saving – due to the fact that I had to file bankruptcy when I was 21. Now, however, I have over a 750 credit score!

If you follow me on YouTube at Bumble Bee Dispatch and/or Facebook at Bumble Bee Dispatch, then you know that I got my start in trucking because of my oldest brother, Corey. Bumble Bee is my company and I named it after my car. Yes, I have a black and yellow "bumble bee" Charger; it's my BAE. Bumble Bee is a one-stop-shop in trucking, brokering, and dispatch.

I hope you guys are ready to read this exciting journey–just one of the chapter's in my life. I guarantee you will not want to put this book down, so go ahead and grab your popcorn, drinks and turn off the TV because this book is amazing, if I do say so myself!

1
High School

Okay, so I'm taking you back to high school where it all started. I began high school at in August 1999 at the age of 14. I attended Jonesboro High School which is about 15 minutes south of downtown Atlanta. The majority of my life. I really loved school and I loved learning. Even to this day, I continue to learn, whether through reading books or watching videos on YouTube. High school was so much different than middle school. It allowed you to be more independent; to make choices. I was able to choose what I wanted to eat for lunch, where I wanted to sit, and what classes I wanted to take, mainly electives. Of course, I had my main classes which were required.

During my first semester in 9th grade, one of my electives was PE. We would have P.E. for half of a semester; the other half, we would take health. One day while in PE, I saw this fine boy named Gerald. I didn't know what grade he was in at the time; I just knew that he was fine. While in P.E., Gerald decides to walk by our class. We were outside the gym practicing CPR on some dummies. He had on this red FUBU shirt and blue jeans (by the way, red was and still is my favorite color). FUBU was "in" at the time and everyone was wearing it. To me, he was "fresh," so I decided to talk to him–to get to know him a little bit better. We talked for a while and he gave me his number.

Notice I said he gave me *his* number. See, I lived with my mom and stepfather and I wasn't allowed to talk to boys on the phone; my stepfather was very strict.

Some days, I felt like Cinderella; I couldn't do anything at home. Other days, I would absolutely dread going home and when I did go home, I would try to stay to myself or in my room.

When school got out later that day, I was riding the school bus home and talking to my friend, Iyesha, I told her that I got Gerald's phone number and couldn't wait to go to *her* house to call him. My mother remarried when I was about eight years old and her husband was very controlling. My mother always said he was bipolar; he would have his good days sometimes, and other times, his days were not so good. When I was 13, I remember we would always go to Shoney's after church. Shoney's was an all you can eat breakfast restaurant. I noticed the restaurant had apartment books near the exit doors. I would look at the apartment books every Sunday and say to myself, "I can't wait until I turn 18 so I can finally move out of my mother's house."

My mother worked a lot and the majority of her customers lived in Alpharetta, north of Atlanta. She had a cleaning business and she was the only employee. Ever since I can remember, the only career my mother had was working for herself. She was a little hustler as well, but I didn't recognize it then. My mother told me how she would work two and three jobs before starting her own cleaning business. I know when she was in her 20s, she worked at Neiman Marcus for a few years, along with other jobs. However, I was born in 1985 and all I've known was the cleaning business.

My father was in and out of my life because he was in and out of prison a lot. I remember when I was younger, my mother would take my brother and I to visit my father in prison. It would bring tears to my eyes because I hated seeing him in there. But, my dad was a hustler as well and always has been; I guess it just ran in the blood.

When I was about five years old, I remember my mom and father getting into an argument. It had something to do with my mother cleaning a home and my dad was supposed to help her with the floors. We arrived at our house and my dad was drunk. We lived in Riverdale, Georgia at that time. My oldest brother, Corey, tried to stop my dad from hitting my mother. Then, out of nowhere, the police arrived. We believed our neighbors called the police. My mother had just purchased, or was in a rent to own plan, a Mercedes Benz from one of her customers. My father got it that vehicle and took off, almost slamming the police officer's hand in the door. Now, they were on a high-speed chase. My dad was in a really bad car accident during the chase and everything was displayed on the news. My mom told me the news had pronounced him dead at the scene, but he was actually airlifted to a hospital and somehow, they were able to save his life. My father was like a vegetable. He had to learn how to talk, walk and do everything all over again.

Back when I was younger, I was used to seeing the police a lot. If it wasn't my dad getting into trouble, then they would be looking for my brother. One night I was in bed asleep and I woke up to an officer flashing a light in my face looking for Corey. I cried a lot back then because I was so young and I didn't understand much, but boy, did we have a lot of drama going on. It would hurt me because I hated seeing my father or brother locked up in prison. I loved my brother very much. Snce he was 12 years older than me, he was a father figure to me.

Once my father's health was better, they returned him back to prison, again, due to the fact that he had attempted to get away from the police, plus he had other charges related to the high-speed chase. Back into the system he went. Visiting my dad in prison was a horrible experience but I would always try to hold the pain inside. I always wanted my dad. Despite his troubles, my father was really cool and laid back. He wasn't strict at all and would let me do pretty much whatever I wanted. I believe that everyone has good in them somewhere. There are a lot of people that will judge a book by its cover, but you can't. I did have great times with my dad. Like when I was around four years old, I remember him taking me in the kitchen and teaching me how to cook eggs and pancakes. Those were the good times. I also remember my father being released from prison. After his release, my dad received a lump sum of money some kind of way. I guess it was from the accident, but I'm not really sure. But, anyway, he took us to Disney World and bought me all kinds of toys.

I believe my mother fell out of love with my father, and after that trip, I didn't see him much until I was about 12 years old. As I stated earlier, I was around eight when my mother remarried. Ronald was my stepfather and marrying him, to me, was the worst mistake ever!

Iyesha was one of my best friends. We did just about everything together, from hanging out and going shopping to just having fun. The first time I spoke to Gerald on the phone, I had butterflies in my stomach. I learned that he was a junior; I was a freshman. He also had a car so he would drive to school. Back then, all the boys had that "beat" in their cars. The beat included huge speakers, an amplifier and maybe a subwoofer. When they played the music, their truck would be beating. It was so cool. And, yes, Gerald had the beat, and I loved it!

As we talked on the phone, he told me about growing up in Detroit, Michigan with his grandmother, Ozie. When he was about 11 years old, he moved with his mother in Riverdale. He was 11 when his father died of a heart attack. We talked for about an hour that day and then he had to go to work. Gerald worked at McDonald's, so we agreed to just talk at school the next day. After I hung up the phone with him, it felt as if my heart fluttered. No one ever knew what I was going through at home because I was always taught to keep everything inside, and my mom used to tell me not to tell her business to my grandmother.

I loved my grandmother so much. She was so sweet and very loving. My grandmother would always give me compliments and encourage me. She would tell me how beautiful I was and always uplift my spirits. When I was younger, I would go to school from my grandmother's house in Southwest Atlanta (now known as the SWATS). I attended Continental Colony Elementary School, right up the street from Tyler Perry Studios–his first studio location in Atlanta. The bus stop was on the corner of my grandmother's house. I remember coming home from school and she would have the front door open with the screen door closed and she would watch me get off the bus.

My grandmother loved to cook. We would have three meals a day. She was a real housewife; not what you see on TV today. She had worked in the past, but during this time, she took care of the house and her grandkids. My grandmother had five children. My Uncle Henderson was the oldest, my mother came next, then my aunties Octavia, Wanda and Tammie. Our family was pretty big.

When I got off the school bus and in the house, my grandmother would ask me what I wanted to eat. I don't know what it was, but I always wanted toast with jelly on it. I didn't like peanut butter and jelly– only jelly toast.

My grandmother was my heart and her name was Naomi Marie. I attended Continental Colony until about the 3rd grade. My mother and grandmother got into an argument and my mom took me out of the school and enrolled me in E.J. Swint Elementary School in Clayton County.

I hated going there because I was used to my old school and friends. That wasn't the only reason. I was only eight years old at the time and I would have to go home by myself and stay there until my mother got home from work. Sometimes, I would get hungry and would be there by myself all day and sometimes, all night, so I had to learn how to cook.

It's amazing how far I have come because now with trucking, I want to help others achieve what I have been able to achieve at such a young age.

I remember hearing noises and hiding under my bed. We didn't have cell phones then, or people didn't use them as much. If they had a cell phone, it was a huge brick one. Most people used pagers, but my mom didn't have either, so I would just have to wait until she got home or until she called me from one of her customer's homes. The more I stayed home by myself, the more I got used to it. As the years went by, it started to feel normal.

So, after meeting Gerald in high school, I guess you could say, I was looking for something that I felt I was lacking–love, because it was something I didn't get at home. I'm not saying my mother didn't love me; of course she did. She did the best she could with what she knew how to do as a parent. My mother worked hard to provide for us, but that was part of the problem–she always worked.

Iyesha and I talked for a little while at her house and I told her about the conversation Gerald and I had. I didn't want it to get too late so after we finished chit chatting, I walked home. It was about a five-minute walk from my house to hers. We lived on the same street but at different ends of the street.

The events and things I went through, I feel a girl should never have to experience. My mom did the best she could to her ability and I knew she loved me, although I may not have always understood her reasoning.

The next day at school when Gerald and I saw each other, he asked me to sit by him at the lunch table. We had the same period for lunch, so from that day on, we would sit together during lunch. We started talking more and learning more about each other and before we knew it we were going together. Yep, we were boyfriend and girlfriend. We would go to the movies and Six Flags and have so much fun. I would have to sneak out of the house most of the time, or I would tell my mom I was going to Iyesha's house and then Gerald would meet me around the corner so I could go with him. I felt like I was in heaven. It was a getaway from my reality. Two months into my freshman year of high school, a dramatic event happened that changed my life forever.

While sitting on the couch in the living room watching TV, talking on the phone and doing my homework all at the same time (basically, what your typical teenager does at 14), my mother yells to me, "Courtney, dinner's ready." I replied, "Ok, mom. I'll be there in a minute."

A few minutes go by and I hadn't made it to the kitchen to eat yet. My stepfather comes in the living room with his belt hanging from his pants and says, "Didn't you hear what your mother said. You need to come in the kitchen now."

I got off the phone, put my homework up and just did what he said so there wouldn't be any chaos. He was used to provoking me and I had to deal with it because I was only 14 and didn't have anywhere to go. Besides, my mother has to take care of me right? Or so I thought.

While I was fixing my plate, he said, "You were about two seconds away from getting your butt beat. I replied, "You're not my father." I guess that really pissed him off because he started yelling even more.

The thing is, my father has never put his hands on me. Although he isn't perfect, my dad has never even whooped me. My father was more of a cool dad (not saying that it's good to be a cool dad), but he didn't discipline me at all. My father was more of a talker and he would talk to me all the time. I made the honor roll every year; always did what I was supposed to do.

I'm thinking in my head how this man can beat me like he says he would for not wanting to eat at a certain time. I sat down and ate my food, but I felt so disgusted sitting there. I hated living there and my mother didn't say anything. I tried to hurry up and eat just so I could leave. I hated being in his presence.

When I finished eating, I got up from the table to empty out my plate. My stepfather said, "Sit down and ask for permission to get up from the table." At this point, I'm like this dude is literally crazy. I continued to empty out my plate in the trash can, washed it and the utensils and proceeded to my room. As I started to walk up the stairs, my stepfather came behind me and started hitting me with his belt, all because I didn't ask for permission to get up from the table. Remember when I told you I felt like Cinderella in that household? Now you see why. The bad part was he actually hit me in my face with his belt. Not sure if he meant to hit my face, but he did. He was slinging his belt everywhere toward me with so much malice. For a while, my mother just sat at the table like nothing happened. I actually had kind of like a slash going across my face. I started screaming and yelling, "I HATE YOU!"

I was trying to get away and make it to my room. When I made it upstairs, finally, my mother went to him and said, "You don't hit my daughter." I'm like, "Mom it's too late. He already did the damage, but thanks for coming now." Then she told me to go call my father. When I ran to get the phone, my father answered in enough time to hear what was going on. My stepfather snatched the phone from my hand and said,

"You have to ask for permission to use the phone." He and my mother were just yelling at each other while I was crying.

Once my father arrived, I felt safe. My father looked pissed when he saw me because of the bruises that were on my face and legs. If my father was like his old self, he probably would've went to jail as well. My father took me to the Clayton County Police Station where they took pictures of me. I had bruises everywhere. I was so hurt on the inside because my mother didn't protect me, and that wasn't the first time she didn't. I was lost, alone and confused. I didn't have any one but Gerald. I believe that is what made us grow closer to each other. My father had also remarried and would go out of town for work, so he was hardly ever at home.

After this incident, my father took me back to my mother's house to get some clothes. I felt so neglected. I couldn't believe I was the one leaving the house. What about this man who abused me? Why isn't he leaving? He did go to jail but got right back out.

I stayed out of school for a week because the scar on my face had to heal. It would hurt when I tried to open my eyes or whenever there was bright light. During this time, it was hard for me to understand. I had mixed feelings about everything. As I've said, in my early childhood, my father was in and out of jail. My dad sold and used drugs and would beat my mother, but he had totally changed at this point in my life. He was there for me. It meant a lot to me because I felt like I could count on him was so happy he came to rescue me. I didn't care about his past or what he used to do, which would be a whole other story. My brother, Corey, who taught me about the trucking business was like my father figure though, especially when my father was away in prison. Corey would watch after me and when I was in middle school, he bought me shoes and clothes and gave me money.

When this incident happened with my stepfather, Corey was heavy in the streets of Atlanta. He was a big time drug dealer and was actually facing federal cases, but we had no idea the feds were after him then. My brother had always been in trucking and loved it. While at my father's house, he was working a job that required him to be out of town most of the time. My father is from Perry Holmes, which used to be one of the projects in Atlanta. He is very intelligent and builds computers from scratch. Back in his day, he was a producer of a TV show that was kind of like Soul Train. My father has always been smart. He knows everything about computers and has so much wisdom. I guess that's why I love my computer so much. Again I come from two hustlers so it really is in my DNA.

I stayed at my father's house for about three months. Some nights at my dad's house I would cry to myself and also pray to God. I asked God to please help me understand why my mother allowed a man to physically abuse me and he still lives there while I'm with my dad. "God, please give me strength to go to school every day and not breakdown and cry," I would pray. I was hurting on the inside, but I continued to walk with a smile and no one ever knew what was going on unless I told them. I would listen to music to ease my pain.

We had to go to court about the incident with my stepfather. When I walked in the courtroom and saw my mother sitting right beside my stepfather, I looked at my dad and said, "Dad, why is she sitting with him after he hit me? Why isn't she with me?" My father said, "Baby I don't know."

We sat down in court and right before the judge gave my stepfather his sentence my mother said, "Wait. Please don't take him to jail because he pays the bills."

That hurt me even more because I knew eventually I would have to live in the same house with that man again. The judge only sentenced him to weekend jail. I made a promise to myself in that courtroom. I prayed to God and said, "Lord, I want to be independent and never want a man to take care of me because if he does, I would have to allow any and everything. God, please make me an independent woman."

It's amazing when you ask for something in life how it may happen, maybe not right then, but eventually it comes around. Sometimes we may think God doesn't hear our voices, but he does I didn't understand because my mom had her own business and she was making good money. She was always independent. Because my mom never really had a relationship with her real father (he and my grandmother divorced when my mother was a little girl), maybe, she, too, was seeking something from men.

My mother would put a man before her kids and it hurt. My stepfather was a computer programmer and he was making over 100K a year over. When we left the courthouse, I couldn't believe what I heard. At that time, no one at school knew what was going on except for Iyesha. But, again, I just played like everything was ok and continued to go to school as normal.

I returned home about three months later, but when I would get off the school bus, I would go to Iyesha's house to wait for my mom to come home. I remember calling her to see if she was there because I didn't want to be alone in the home with my stepfather and my mother says "Girl, you can go home. He ain't going to do nothing to you." She said it as if nothing had happened. She never asked me how I felt, if I was ok, or anything. I guess it was just a part of life and I had to just be tough and suck it up. Things happen, right? I guess that's the normal life of a 14-year-old. That situation did make me stronger. Like they say, what don't kill you, will only make you stronger. I was built for this, so yeah, it molded me into being stronger and tougher.

Dating Gerald eased my mind of all the stress I had going on. When I turned 15, I wanted a job so bad. I applied at McDonald's–not the same one Gerald worked at, but the one a little closer to my house. They hired me and I was so happy because now I could make my own money. After two weeks of working there, they told me they made a mistake because I was only 15 years old and you had to be 16 to work there. I told the lady that the person who hired me saw my ID and hired me anyway. She apologized and said I couldn't work there until I turned 16. I was even more determined to get a job so I could buy what I wanted. When I went home, I came up with the idea to change the date on my birth certificate. I made a copy of my birth certificate and changed the 1985 to 1984 with whiteout and made another copy of it. I went to Food Depot, a grocery store in Riverdale. They only needed a copy of my birth certificate and Social Security card. They hired me and I was so happy.

I worked ALL the time—overtime, weekends, on off days; I didn't care. I was now able to get my hair done when I wanted and I bought my own school clothes. I felt independent for a 15-year-old and didn't have to ask my mother for anything because I had my own funds.

Gerald and I would talk about life after high school and he told me he wanted to join the military. We talked about getting married and having a family. Gerald and I were very close. He was my escape from all the drama and stress. We had been dating for over a year and were also sexually active.

Corey was 27 years old and in the streets as usual. We are 12 years apart. My father was still working and we would talk from time to time. Gerald and I would spend as much time together as we could. I was now in 10th grade and he was a senior. We went to the prom together and when it was time for him to leave for the military, I didn't want him to go. I knew it would only be a short period of time after basic training and school training that he'd get stationed somewhere. He was actually stationed at Fort Stewart in Hinesville, GA. It is about three hours south of Atlanta, not too far from Savannah. I would drive down to where he was on the weekends or he would come up here. We would see each other usually twice a month on weekends. Corey bought me a car when I turned 16. We went to the auction together and he bought it for me. I loved my brother because he would always come through for me when I needed him the most. At 16 with a car and a job, boy was I something else! I was happier than ever.

Gerald and I took a trip to Myrtle Beach, SC with some friends. I believe it was there in Myrtle Beach where I got pregnant with our daughter Shimiya, at 16.

About a month after returning from Myrtle Beach, my period didn't come on and YES, I was scared as HELL. My mother and stepfather eventually separated and he no longer lived in the house. Iyesha and I went to the Health Department because they gave FREE pregnancy tests. We went to the one in Forest Park and I remember when the lady told me I was pregnant. She signed me up for something called WIC and Medicaid. I still didn't know how I was going to announce this to my mother.

So, when I got home, I said, "Mom, guess what?

She was going through her mail and asked, "What?"

I replied, "I got WIC."

She looked and me and asked, "What do you mean, you have WIC? You can only get WIC if you're pregnant."

I said, "Yes, I got WIC."

My mother asked, "Are you pregnant?"

I replied, "YES."

To be honest, my mother wasn't mad at me and I was shocked. See, my mom had my brother, Corey, when she was 16 years old as well. She came to me and said, "Courtney, it will be ok and I'm here for you." That right there showed me that my mother loved me. She may have had her own way of showing it, but I'm glad she wasn't mad at me for being pregnant.

When I broke the news to Gerald, he was happy and so was I. He was hesitant about telling his mother the news because he knew that she would be upset because she had plans for him to join the military and make something of his life which I can understand. That is what a normal parent would want.

When he finally broke the news to his mother, she was so upset. She called my mother and told her I should have an abortion because I'm only 16 and too young to have a baby. My mother didn't believe in abortions. I guess because she too was in my shoes and had not aborted my brother. My mother and Gerald's mom got into an argument over the situation and my mom told her, "I'm not letting my daughter have No Abortion!" That was the end of that "convo."

I remember talking to my friend Samantha and asking her what I should do. She said, "Courtney, do what you feel is best."

So I decided to keep my child. I continued to go to school every day pregnant and all, but I had determination. I wasn't going to give up. I kept striving. I was determined I was going to be successful, even when there were hard times or when I didn't think there was a light at the end of the tunnel. I had to keep pushing and have faith. This only made me stronger. See, I thought what in the world was I doing, not knowing this was just another part of life's lessons.

What I was experiencing, was building me to be tough. Having a baby at 16 makes you want to hustle to have the best for your child. You have to work even harder because now you have someone who is depending on you. If I fail in life, then I'm failing her and I couldn't let her down. I would talk and sing to Shimiya while she was in my belly. Gerald would call because at this time, he is in IRAQ fighting in the war. I would put the phone to my belly so he could speak with his daughter. I was now in 12th grade, 17 years old and five months "prego. "

Life will hit you with trials and tribulations. No matter what you go through, it is only bracing you for what the future holds. Sometimes we can't understand the things we go through and we ask GOD, "Why me, Lord?" I know I have several times.

I've learned over the years how to forgive and forgive again and again. Being 16 and -pregnant, I didn't give up. I kept going to school and I also graduated high school on time.

Mothers, please show your kids love and NEVER EVER put a man before your child. If that man ever leaves you, your kids may be all you have. The same goes for men. Please be present in your kids' life. Boys and girls need their mother and father. It takes both parents to raise a child. Be there for them, so they won't have to look for love elsewhere and end up with a child, like I did.

Typically, most girls who get pregnant at a young age are missing something from home or have experienced something horrible in or outside of the home. See, I was molested by my stepbrother when I was eight years old. He was my stepfather's son ---- -from another woman. I never told my immediate family, but my mom knows. My life was so chaotic back then. I'm glad that chapter of my life is over. I hope that I can continue to help other girls who find themselves in similar situations. My mother is a great person. It was the man in her life that altered her thinking.

If you're a young girl reading this book, remember to love yourself even if no one else does. If you're an older woman, keep your head up. I know you've been hurt, but don't allow your pain to make you bitter or change your spirit. Remember, we only get one life, so let's make the best of it.

2
Life or Death: Preeclampsia – Eclampsia

"OUCH!"

"Courtney, what's wrong with you?" my mother asked.

"Ma, my feet hurt. Every time I walk on them, they hurt and they are swelling. Ma, I'm only six months. Don't your feet start swelling when it's time to have the baby? Why are my feet swelling now?

My mom replied "Yes, you're right. They do swell when it's close to time to have the baby. I don't know why they are swelling, but if you keep having pain we will have to take you to the doctor."

"Ok Ma, but I'm going to look it up on the computer."

I got up off the couch in the living room and walked upstairs to my room to get on the computer. Every time I took a step, the pain was excruciating. I had to see what was going on with my body. I knew I had some stress, but could stress cause all of this? Corey and I had just got into an argument because he wanted to borrow the car he bought for me. Even though he bought me the car I really didn't mind him driving it, but I was kind of feeling myself. I mean, I was a senior in high school and I couldn't ride the bus. I told him I needed it to drive to school and he went from zero to 100 real quick.

I also felt as if I was dealing with this pregnancy by myself. My daughter's father was in the army fighting the war in Iraq and I was here in the states waiting to have our beautiful baby girl. This was the year 2002. Again, I loved computers; my father built me my first computer. So, I went online and typed in feet swelling on the site, Web MD. It advised if it swelling persisted in your hands and feet you could have something called preeclampsia. The name itself scared me so I typed it in and believe it or not, all of the symptoms I was experiencing were symptoms of preeclampsia. It is a high blood pressure disorder. Some symptoms included heart palpations, shortness of breath, protein in urine and high blood pressure. The website also stated that if symptoms get worse, it could lead to eclampsia which causes a seizure, stroke or coma. Whew! Boy, was I scared to death. I immediately ran downstairs and told my mother what I read. She couldn't believe her eyes and said, "I'm just going to take you to the hospital tomorrow."

I was scared and nervous at the same time, but I'm glad I had the sense to use the computer to find out what was going on with me before it was too late. I've heard of stories of women dying during pregnancy and childbirth and some of those women had preeclampsia.

We arrived at the doctor's office the next day, checked in and sat in the waiting room. I was really nervous and was looking at my mom like, my feet are just swelling and hands but what do you think the doctor is going to say? Next thing I know they called my name, Courtney Petty.

When the nurse sat me down in the chair, she told me she needed to check my blood pressure and to relax. After she checked my blood pressure, her eyes got really big and she said, "Let me check your blood pressure again to make sure I'm reading this right."

Now she literally just scared the shit out of me. My blood pressure was 160/100. She then told me to go and urinate in a cup. When I finished, just like Web MD stated, there was protein in my urine. I guess you already know what happened next–they were sending me to the emergency room.

At this time, I'm 17 years old and only 26 weeks pregnant. It was September 17, 2002. My daughter wasn't due until December of that year, so having the baby was the least thing I was thinking about. However, I wasn't sure and was scared and nervous.

My mom took me to the emergency room and she sat there with me for a little while, but she had to leave because, of course, she had to work. I also had a little brother, Brandon, who was about 8 years old at that time, so she needed to go attend to him.

I was at the hospital all alone. My daughter's father was in the military and we were at war with IRAQ. Later that night, a doctor came into my room to tell me they were going to have to give me a steroid shot just in case I have my child early, so her lungs can start developing. I agreed to it because I wanted to do what was best for my baby.

When I woke up the next morning, I felt like I was the nutty professor. I had blown up overnight. Remember, I was already swelling and the steroid shot just made it worse. I was huge. My breasts were enlarged and my butt. My father called me around 3:00 PM on September 18th and said, "I'm coming to the hospital. What do you want to eat?" I told him to get me something from Chick-fil-a. After we hung up the phone, I decided to get up and take a shower because I had been sitting in the bed for a day without a bath and I wanted to clean myself up. When I got up and went to the bathroom, I noticed my balance seemed off and my body seemed a little different. While looking in the mirror, my hand curved up really tight and I fell on the bathroom floor. It was like I blacked out because that's all I remembered!

SURPRISE! When I finally woke up in my hospital bed from the blackout, my whole family was in my hospital room. I was out of it. I didn't know what was going on and why they had an oxygen mask over my face.

I remember my Aunt Tammie saying congratulations. I looked at her with this confused look on my face and said, "Congratulations for what?"

She said, "You just had a baby."

"I didn't have no baby. What are you talking about?"

Everyone was looking like what's wrong with Courtney. See, when I fell out on the bathroom floor, I didn't know until later that my preeclampsia had turned into eclampsia and I'd had a seizure. The doctors had to do an emergency C-section to get the baby out or I would have died. My father was the first person to arrive at the hospital because he was coming to bring me some food. The doctors told him the nurse found me on the bathroom floor and that I had a seizure so they had to do an emergency C-section. Once again, my father came through and I'm glad he did and that he was there while I was out of it.

When he did arrive, they'd told him I might not make it and explained to him what had happened. My dad told me I was in ICU and he called my mother, who was at work in Alpharetta cleaning a customer's house. I'm not sure how long I was out of it, but I do know when I woke up, everyone was there. Maybe they were afraid that something could've happened to me as well. Corey even showed up. It felt good because we had just had an argument and maybe it could have raised my blood pressure some. He came to the hospital with a teddy bear and balloons. He was my rock.

I do believe that GOD kept me here for a reason. Now back to the conversation with my auntie. Honestly, I was on so much medication that I felt as if I'd just went to sleep and woke up. I kept trying to take that oxygen mask off and my mom kept putting it back on my face. When my aunt told me I had just had the baby, I lifted up my gown and saw the staples across my bikini area and I said, "OH, I did have a baby." I know reading this it may sound weird and crazy, but falling out on the hospital floor and waking up with all kinds of medication would have any one going crazy.

After some of the medicine wore off, I was getting back to my normal self again. The next day was so much better, but what I had just experienced, I told my mom I never want to go through that again. My body felt as if a firetruck had just hit it. I remember my Aunt Tavi sitting in the hospital room with me one day and I believe she told me I was lucky. It made me feel good that she sat and talked with me. I also had visits from some of my best high school buddies Andrea and Stevette. We used to all hang together and go out and have fun. Those were the good old days.

After being in the hospital for a day or so, I was ready to go home, especially after lying in that uncomfortable bed. And, people would be in and out of the hospital room throughout the day and night so I couldn't get any rest. I just wanted to go home and be in my own bed. The nurses gave me popsicles and said that that my blood pressure had to go down before I could go home. They also rolled me down in a wheelchair so I could visit my daughter, Shimiya. She was in an incubator wrapped in plastic and her body was transparent. She only weighed 15 ounces–not even a pound. I had her at 26 weeks pregnant. She was on an oxygen machine and it seemed to me like she was in so much pain. I would read to her and talk to her so she could hear my voice. Every day I would pray that she makes it. She was a fighter.

When I was able to go home I remember the doctors giving me Percocet for pain. That is a really strong medication. It had me hallucinating and seeing spots. Most of the time, I would sleep when I came home. After about a week of taking the medication, my arm started shaking in the middle of the night. I was scared and started screaming for my mom. I was sleeping in her bed and she said, "I'm taking you off that medication and will start giving you natural stuff to take. That medication is causing you to have those symptoms. You're not taking it anymore." So I stopped taking the pain medication and the hallucination and shaking went away. After about two weeks I felt like I was back to normal even though I knew my body was still healing.

A few weeks later, I went back to high school and continued taking my classes as usual. I would go to school and get out early to go to work. They had a program at school where you could leave early to work and since the majority of my credits were completed, I participated in that program so I could work and make some money before Shimiya came home.

Shimiya was still in the hospital and had to stay there for three months before she was able to come home. Right around Christmas time Shimiya came home and was four pounds. After the Christmas break was over, Shimiya had to go to daycare and I went back to school.

A few months went by and it was time for graduation. I was happier than ever because I overcame the odds. Most people probably thought that being 16 and pregnant, I wouldn't finish high school. WELL, I proved them wrong. I was my mother's first child to graduate high school. I was proud that even though I got pregnant and had a baby, I was able to graduate from high school.

My mom was never really big on throwing me any parties, so I didn't have a graduation party. I went to a few of my friends graduation parties, though. My father wasn't able to attend my graduation, he had remarried and had to watch his stepdaughter's kids. However, my lovely grandma, Naomi was there with my granddaddy, George, all of my aunties, my Uncle Kooch, my cousins, and of course, my mom.

Now that graduation was over and done with, it was time for our senior trip to Cancun, Mexico. Yes! I was so glad I was able to go. One of my besties, Andrea, also went and boy did we have the time of our lives. We walked the strip, went to all types of clubs and took a boat ride. Even though I was having so much fun, I was homesick. I missed my baby, Shimiya. Her father had also returned home from the war in Iraq, so I was eager to get back to see him as well. It had been one whole year and I couldn't wait.

I called my mom from Mexico and she called Gerald on thee-way. Our seven-day trip seemed like forever. Once we got back on the plane to head home, I was so ecstatic. I just couldn't wait to return. My mother picked us up from the airport and we headed home. The next day Gerald, Shimiya, and I got dressed and went to the mall to take pictures. We spent all the time we could together before he had to return to Fort Stewart. He made a promise that he would try to come up every weekend or every other weekend to see us. I also told him I would drive down as well when I could.

Ladies, it's very important that you take care of your bodies, especially when pregnant. Listen to your body and if you feel that something isn't right, then please get it checked while you can–it can save your life and your child's life.

Stress can also cause many health issues, so try to stay calm and happy. Please google -preeclampsia to learn more about it.

Pregnancy can have complications, but it's up to you to make sure you do all you can to decrease those chances. I had a cousin who passed away from toxemia after giving birth to her daughter.

To be honest, since this was my first pregnancy, I had no idea what contractions felt like or how it feels when your water breaks. It was like I just went to sleep and woke up with a baby.

3
Life After High School

After graduating from high school, I was going to go straight to college. Well, at least that was my plan. However, my mother asked, "Courtney, why don't you take up a trade first? That way you don't have to worry about going to college and trying to work a job and take care of a child." She suggested that I go to school for medical billing and coding and then I could work from home and still be there with my daughter. She had a valid point so that's what I did.

I went to Georgia Medical Institute for medical billing and coding. It was a five-month program. I also worked on the weekends as a receptionist at United Nissan in Morrow. While attending the institute, I thought I'd graduate and start making money right away. NOPE! I graduated from Georgia Medical and every place I went in search of a job, I was told that I had to have five years of experience or more. Bullshit. I was so pissed. I attended this school, graduated from this school and now I have student loans. They didn't accept the Hope Scholarship of which I qualified for, so I had to take out loans with Sallie Mae and soon I was going to have to start paying those loans back. What did I get myself into? I was feeling down but I couldn't let that stop me because I have a child to take care of so I got to make this work for us. Gerald, was still stationed at Fort Stewart and we would see each other most weekends.

Since the medical billing career didn't work out, I decided to go back to my first choice– college. (I was left with a diploma and I wasn't working from home as I thought would be the case). I enrolled in Atlanta Metropolitan College. Math was and has always been my favorite subject, so I chose to major in accounting. And, since I loved helping people and solving problems, I decided to minor in psychology. I liked both of the fields and so that's what I went with. I was still working at United Nissan on weekends but I was only making around $10 an hour. Working about 8 hours, my check was only $80. I knew we couldn't survive off of this money and that eventually, I would need to get another job.

I loved going to school because I always loved learning. School was fun and I met a lot of amazing people. First semester, we went to the bookstore to get our books and those books were very heavy. As I was leaving the bookstore, all of my books fell out of the box they gave me right onto the ground. I was embarrassed, but there was this nice gentleman who came over and picked my books up for me and took them to my car. Jabari was his name. He became one of my best friends over the years. I always looked at him like a big brother. He would give me advice on different things and would also help me move when I moved from apartment to apartment.

I signed up with the temporary agency, Angelyn Staffing in Mcdonough. At that time, I was still living in Riverdale with my mother. My first job through the temp service was at the Dunkin Donuts Distribution Center. I only made $9.00 at 40 hours a week; much better than bringing home $80 a week. Since I had to work daytime hours, I went to school at night and on the weekend. After three months, they hired me permanently and my pay increased by 50 cents. My friends and I would go and hang out in the Buckhead area. Even though we were young, we would still get into the clubs. I would hang out with my friends Iyesha, Candace, Andrea and Stevette. Trying to manage college, work, a child, and a social life was too much on my plate at 18. I needed more money because I had bills to pay and something just had to give. .

I tried selling AVON, but there were so many people selling AVON. I was never able to make it as far as they promised on those videos you watch where people were living their life and driving their dream cars. I made sales with AVON, but I knew there was more out there available to me.

I remember going to this strip club one day and I wanted to be a waitress. I would hear from other girls in college who were waitresses that they would make good money in tips. I decided to be a waitress because I would be able to go home every night with a paycheck, plus the guys at the strip club were just throwing their money away. I was also too scared and too shy to dance. So, being a dancer was the last thing on my mind. But, when I went there, I told them I was in college and I just wanted to be a waitress. The owner said all of their waitresses danced, too. Well, say no more. I politely left the club and decided that I will need to just get two jobs and put school on hold for a little while.

That's exactly what I did. I asked the temp service to find me another job at Benton Express. Benton Express was a trucking company and I worked there at night doing billing for them. I had no idea that I would have a career in trucking. I learned about BOL (Bill of Lading) and submitting invoices. They paid $10 an hour. I would work there at night and Dunkin Donuts during the daytime.

I dropped out of college because I couldn't work two jobs, go to school and be there for my daughter. Something had to go, so I let college go. My mother did help me out with my daughter. I don't know how I would've done it without her. I can say she was in my corner.

Even though the income was a little better, it still wasn't enough. Leaving one job and going to the next, by the time I made it home, I was completely exhausted. I would often say, "GOD, there has to be a better life for me than this." I had to pay my car note, insurance, cell phone bill, gas and more, plus take care of my daughter. After taxes, there wasn't much money left, but I kept pushing.

I would still see Gerald some weekends, but our relationship was dwindling away. We went through what most couples go through and at 20 (Gerald was 22), we ended our relationship and went our separate ways. It was hard to let go and move on, at first. I really loved him. But, time heals all wounds and as the weeks, days and months went by, it became much easier. I will always love Gerald because he was my first true love.

My stepfather passed away. My little brother, Brandon, was around 11 years old and it was really hard on him losing his dad. Although my stepfather wasn't my favorite cup of tea, I still attended the funeral out of respect. I was about 20 years old around this time. He and my mother were still married, but separated at the time of his passing. He had already moved on with another woman named Laura. He planned to divorce my mother and I think they had already started the process because he was already making wedding plans with his new girlfriend. My mother paid for the funeral, but the girlfriend had the nerve to pull up to the funeral like she was already the MRS when my mother's divorce from him wasn't even final. My stepfather had three or four other "bay mommas" who also attended the funeral, so I guess you can imagine how everything turned out without me having to say too much.

I felt sorry for my little brother, Brandon, because he now had to grow up without his father. Many African American kids already don't have a father or father figure in their lives to begin with. My mother had life insurance. One thing I can say is she has always been business minded. She strongly believed in having a life insurance policy. And, she strongly encouraged me to get life insurance policies on my daughter's father and I couldn't understand why; I was only 20 years old. I would tell my mother that he's in the army and in great shape. He works out every day and besides, I'm only 20 and he's 22. We didn't need life insurance now. She would say, "Courtney, you could get a one million dollar policy for only $20 a month because he was so young." I wasn't listening to that. Shoot, I already had enough bills as it was and I was not trying to take on any more.

I wish I would've listened to my mom. I am now a licensed life insurance representative and I try to teach others about the importance of life insurance and help them to open and maintain life insurance policies.

I started applying for jobs because the distribution center I was working for was relocating to Florida. We had to either move to Florida or find new jobs. I applied for a few banks online. Bank of America hired me and I was so happy. I loved working for them. I started off in lockbox and it was there where I met Shelly. She was about three years older than me, but really cool. She knew all of the hang out spots and she basically took me out of my shell. There were times where I didn't want to leave the house and she would say, "Girl, we're going out so put your clothes on." I loved her for that because although I wouldn't want to go, once I did, I was glad to get out of the house. Shelly and I did everything together. We talked on the phone all the time, we went shopping together and just did the normal girly stuff. Shelly was a really good friend–the type of friend who would pick you up when you're feeling down and always make sure we were slaying wherever we would go. If my hair or wig wasn't right, she would fix it. If she didn't like my outfit, she would give me one of hers to wear.

We both worked at the bank on the weekends starting out and would come in sometimes during the weekday to help out as needed. After being in lockbox for only a few months, I got a teller position at the same bank. YAY! I was so happy. I started working as a teller at a Fayetteville branch and it was really awesome. We would have to do so many referrals each day. But I met some amazing people there like Keisha Knight Pulliam (Rudy from the Cosby Show) and other actors and athletes who would come into the branch to do they're normal banking. I loved working for Bank of America. I received awards for my accomplishments. Everyone there was overly nice. We were like a great big family.

Something dramatic happened in my life while I was working there which caused me to go into a deep depression that I actually had to quit working at the bank. There was no reason for me to leave, but because of what I was dealing with at the time, I had no choice. I turned in my bank keys and that was it. After about a month or so, I hated that I left and I prayed that I find another job in banking. When I say GOD is an awesome GOD, I really do mean that. Five months later, I received a position with Wachovia (now Wells Fargo). I started in lockbox with Wachovia and was making $9.50 an hour. I was glad that I was working again and was able to return to banking.

No matter what obstacles you face in life, you have to keep pushing if you want better. Sometimes the journey may seem hard but remember it's only temporarily. Stay strong, have faith and keep pushing. Don't get discouraged when faced with tough situation;-- - just know that you are being molded.

I actually now like pressure because it only makes me stronger. Like they say, what don't kill you, will only make you stronger. I've met some amazing people on the many -jobs I've had.

For all of my young and/or single moms out there, I know it gets hard and sometimes you want to give up. Just always remember that if I can do it, you can to. Keep your head up, stay focused, grind and hustle.

Figure out what you're good at and what you can do to earn extra income. There's nothing wrong with having a side hustle to earn extra income. In fact, if you're someone who wants more out of life, I want you to write down on a sheet of paper all of your skills–everything you're good at. Once finished, think about what type of business you could start. Think outside the box! Follow us on social media and when I come to a city near you, I want to see some of your great ideas. Who knows? I may even help fund some of the business ideas. Stay positive, invest in yourself and your future.

4
The Central Station

"By you a Drank" by T-Pain playing on V-103, the Free Money Station

*"Snap ya fingers, do the step, you can do it all by yourself
Woo, baby girl, what's your name?
Let me talk to you, let me buy you a drink*

*I'm a buy you a drank (Then I'm a take you home with me)
I got money in the bank (Shawty, what chu think about that? Find me in the gray Cadillac)*

"It's going down tonight at the Central Station. Come through."

I was driving to work one Friday morning listening V-103, the *free money station*. After they finished playing my song, T-Pain's *Buy You a Drank,* I decided to call one of my besties, Candace, to see if she wanted to go out tonight after work. Candace and I have been friends since the 8th grade middle school. The phone rang and rang. I was thinking in my head, "Come on girl, pick up. We need to step out tonight.

"Hello," Candace finally answered.

"What's up girl?" I asked.

"Nothing. At work," Candace replied.

"Listen, when you get off work today, we need to go get us a fit and get our nails done so we can hit up the Central Station. You know that spot is popping every Friday night, girl."

Candace and I were like Bonnie and Clyde. She was down for whatever. I would have Candace all over the "A" (Atlant) and we would have a blast.

"Ok. That's a bet," Candace responded. "I'll meet you tonight at your house."
"Ok, boo. Talk to you later," I said.

Every time Candace and I stepped out, there was always a photo shoot. I loved my wigs and I would go to the beauty supply store and find the baddest wig. Everyone who knew me, knew I would have the flyest wigs. People would actually ask me to go to the store with them to pick out a wig.

The club was lit when we arrived. Parking was always a nightmare and the line would be wrapped around the building, but it was worth it. The Central Station was like the Walmart of clubs. The inside was big like a Walmart and it seemed like thousands of people could get inside and there would still be enough room to move around. Once we stepped into the building, they were playing *I'm a* Flirt by R Kelly. First, we headed over to the bar to get us a drink. My favorite drink is a Long Island Iced Tea. That drink right there was something else. We got our drinks as began walking through the crowd when all of a sudden, I feel someone tap me on my shoulders. I am not ready to give no one my number or even talk to anyone. I just stepped in the club. I mean give me a min bro. But, when I turned around and saw who approached me, I lost my breath for a second. The guy in front of me was fine as wine. He had the swag of Young Jeezy. He was about 5'10, brown skinned and he actually had pretty eyes. I didn't like or date pretty boys and he wasn't. I could tell he was from the streets, but he was the finest man in the club.

We talked and chatted for a little while then they started playing the son "Shawty" by Plies. I loved Plies and all of his music. I gave him my number and he also put his number in my phone and saved his name as Joe. Candace and I danced, played a little pool and had a great time at the club until it was time for it to close.

I've always had a thing for cars that would be hooked up and I would hook up just about all of my cars, or I would buy them already hooked up. I named my company, Bumble Bee, after my car. After club closed, everyone would post up in the parking lot. I would check out the guys with the flyest cars. I had a thing for street guys back then, I guess because my father is from the streets and so is my brother. That's all I knew. I liked a man who had a little edge to him.

The next day I woke up with a hangover from the Long Island Iced Tea and I didn't remember much about the club, except that we had a good time. I forgot about the guy Joe who put his number in my phone. I called Candace and we chopped it up on the phone for a few and decided to get up later to go shopping.

About a week later, I was scrolling through my phone and I see a number saved as Joe. I had literally forgotten about the guy I met in the club that had put his number in my phone. I kept asking myself, "Who is Joe?" I also didn't remember I texted the message, "Oh, you must not have been interested because you never called or texted me." Next thing I know, my phone started ringing and it was Joe calling me. I looked at my phone like, "Oh, now you want to call." I straight sent him to voicemail. He then responded with a pic. My God! When he sent that pic, I was blowing his phone back up because now I remembered him. We talked for a few minutes, then he told me he would call me tomorrow so we could get up. After we hung up the phone, I had a smile on my face because from his appearance and our convo, he seemed really cool and someone who I would like to get to know better.

The next morning, I woke up, got Shimiya and my niece, Coreyonna (Corey's daughter), dressed. I was going to take them shopping at Underground Atlanta. We arrived at Underground, the kids ate and we went to Footlocker to look for shoes for them. My phone started ringing. When I saw that it was Joe calling, I started to get butterflies in my stomach. There was just something about him. He made me laugh. He asked me if I had a boyfriend. Since I was single at the time, I told him that I hadn't found anyone yet.

Then he says, "So how do I apply?"

I replied, "Huh? Apply for what?"

Joe said, "Apply to be your boyfriend."

I said, "Oh. I don't know. I need to get to know you first."

He said, "Ok, can you meet me later today in Henry County?

I was still living in Riverdale, which is in Clayton County. I told him that we could link up and I would call him back later after I finished shopping.

Shimiya and Yonna found some cute shoes and we walked around downtown for a little bit. Before it was time to go, we got some ice cream and then we headed back home. When we got in the car, the girls went straight asleep. I would take priceless photos as much as I could to send to Corey who was in federal prison. I think my brother went to prison when Coreyonna was only two years old, so he missed out on a lot in her life. I would take his kids to visit him in prison as often as I could.

As I pulled in to the QuikTrip (a popular gas station in Metro Atlanta) waiting to meet Joe, I saw this very nice charger parked in the parking lot. I'd never seen his car, so I didn't know it was his. I called him to see where he was and sure enough, he was the one driving the charger. It was a money green charger, with rims and beat. His charger was super clean and hooked up. I parked my car and when he got out of the car, his swag was on point. He was looking good and smelling good. He seemed to be the perfect gentleman. He asked if I would like to ride around the city so we could talk and get to know each other a little better. I was thinking in my head, of course I would. "Sure," I told him.

When I opened the car door, *Jugg Man* by Young Ralph was playing on the radio. Everyone loved Young Ralph. As we rolled out of the parking lot and headed to downtown Atlanta, the song, *Look Like Money,* was beating. I was extremely happy in that moment with him. I guess I was a hopeless romantic or I just fell in love very easily because I was looking for love at 21.

The men who I really loved, my father and my brother, Corey, were both incarcerated at the time. Corey always looked out for me and tried to be my father when my dad was absent. I remember when my brother was shot by a police officer. I was around eight years old. It scared the living life out of me because I thought he was dead. It was on Channel 5 News. He got into an argument with his baby's mother and she called the police, so my brother took off running, mainly because he had weed on him. The officer who was chasing him told Corey that he would kill him and if my brother had not slightly turned his head, he would be dead and I probably would never been doing anything with trucking.

The news reporter announced that he was taken to taken to Grady Hospital and the tears just kept flowing down my face. I was home alone and couldn't wait for my mom to arrive so I could tell her what had happened. My brother was like my rock and he could do no wrong in my eyes.

My father was locked up on Rice Street in Atlanta, but I couldn't remember why. I do remember going to visit my dad and picking up the phone to talk to him. It was hard for any words to come out of my mouth because the tears would flow first. My father would say, "Courtney, don't cry. I'll be out soon." He didn't understand that I was hurting because I loved him so much and I hated seeing him in there. Even though he was in the county jail, it was still hard on me. My father was a very smart man, although he kept getting caught up in the system. It seemed as if Corey followed his footsteps because he too was in and out of jail as a teen.

Most of the time, I would keep my pain hidden; no one really knew what I was going through. So meeting Joe at this point in my life, took my mind off of reality. He was fun and someone I could talk to. After our ride through the city, he took me back to my car and gave me a hug. On my way home, I kept thinking of him and was ready to see what was going to happen with us later.

I've learned that everything isn't always what it seems; especially when you first meet someone. People will always put their best foot forward until you really get to know them. I've also learned that life has so many variables that you never know what you will get out of it.

The pain that you experience will mold you and shape you either in a good way or a bad way. People may hurt you, but you can't allow that to stop your growth.

See, I was the type of person that held grudges and held on to the painful experiences. This stopped my healing and growth. I was hurt by my father because he was in and out of my life, in and out of prison, physically abused my mother and was a drug user. He is now a changed man but he was supposed to be there to teach me what to look for in a man and how a woman should be treated by a man. I was hurt by my oldest brother because he, too, was in and out of jail, living the fast life so he wasn't a good example of what a man should be or how a man should treat a woman either. Now, he loved his-- family and he was a great provider, but money, women and cars were his priority. My -brother has now changed, but he went through a lot to become the man he is today. I - was hurt by my stepbrother, who molested me when I was eight. He was my stepfather's oldest son. I was hurt by my mother's husband when I was 14. He physically hurt me by beating me, and my father was the only one who came to my rescue. I was hurt by my mother who I felt put a man before her kids. I felt emotionally neglected. Most of my other family including my aunties, grandparents and cousins, never knew the pain I was going through because I never told them. I always held everything inside.

My mom wasn't a very emotional person. I was my mother's first child to graduate from high school. I never had a Sweet 16 party. I never had a graduation party. I've never had a baby shower with any of my kids. My mother did love me and she did the best she could to raise my brothers and I. She's an awesome mom and I wouldn't trade her for anything in the world. We have had talks about the past and she has apologized for her mistakes. With all of the pain I've endured, I found forgiveness.

No one is perfect and we all make mistakes, but it's important that when we do, we ask for forgiveness from the people who were affected. I highly believe that you reap what you sow. My mother and I have a great relationship now and I also have a great relationship with my father.

When you meet someone, let them show you with their actions who they are and don't just make assumptions based on the way things look. It's like judging a book -from its cover. A person can paint a pretty picture, but the inside can be ugly. Please make wise decisions because the decisions you make today, will affect your future.

5
Lollipop Entertainment

Joe and I started seeing a lot more of each other and even after finding out he didn't own a dump truck company like he told me when we first met, I still liked him. He was a ladies man and after dating for two years, we eventually ended our relationship. I was still working for Wells Fargo and ended up moving into an apartment in Stockbridge. My bankruptcy was finally discharged. My deposit for my apartment was $600. I paid it because I felt that filing bankruptcy was a new start for me and I wanted to start rebuilding my credit. I ended up working a second job to help with the bills. It seemed like I just couldn't make enough to keep up with my expenses. I got paid from the bank every two weeks and my check would be less than $800 dollars. My rent was $733 dollars. I had a $400 truck note. Since I filed for bankruptcy, I had to finance a vehicle from a Buy Here, Pay Here location that had sky high interest rates but I had to do what I had to do to rebuild my credit and I needed a vehicle. I also had the normal expenses like utilities, car insurance, credit card bills and groceries, and I also had a four-year-old daughter who was depending on me.

So, I started a new job at the Penalty Box, a sports bar in Stockbridge. After I would get off from the bank, I would go home and shower, then go to the Penalty Box.

I worked as a waitress there and would sometimes bartend on the side. My mother helped me with my daughter, Shimiya. The problem was that sometimes, I didn't get home from work until 2 or 3 AM and I would have to wake up around 6 AM to get ready for my job at Wells Fargo. That meant I only had about 3-4 hours of sleep every night. I would fall asleep just about every day at Wells Fargo. My co-workers would wake me up and I would stay awake for a little while, then dose right off to sleep again. I remember my manager asking if I was ok. I told her that I was just tired and that I don't get much sleep because of my second job and that everything else was ok. Eventually, I had to leave the Penalty Box because the hours weren't working out for me and I couldn't risk my main job which provided benefits.

They say when it rains, it pours and boy did I feel like I was going through a thunderstorm. Every day while driving my truck to work it would shake really hard. I remember calling my dad because he knew all about cars and how to fix them. I told him what the truck was doing and he said that it sounded like I needed new tires. I was like, "I don't have any money to buy no tires." And he said, "Well, if you keep on driving that truck then you can kill yourself on the road."

My father was very good at giving advice; however, he didn't have any money to help me because he was trying to get on his feet himself at 50 years old. He met someone in Florida and had relocated there.

At 22, I felt so alone. I had no money saved in the bank and no one in my family to go to for help. The worst part was my truck eventually ended up shutting down and now I had to pay to get it fixed in addition to paying for rent and the rest of my bills. I remember there were times my daughter and I would have to eat noodle soup for the month because I didn't have any funds left over to buy much food. I felt defeated and wanted to give up.

One day I was getting off from work at the bank and my gas light came on in my truck. I drove a few exits down the road, but I couldn't make it home because I didn't have any gas money. I pulled over to an Exxon station and while sitting in my truck, I just started crying and praying, praying and crying. I was talking to God saying, "Lord, I don't know what I'm going to do." I got paid through direct deposit the next day, but I needed money now to make it home. My bank account was negative as usual before payday, so I couldn't use my bank card to put fuel in the truck. Next thing I know, a man came to my car door out of nowhere. He needed some directions and using my cell phone, I was able to find the location he was looking for on the Internet. The place he was trying to get to was actually right across the street so I guess God had sent me an angel to help me get home. After I found the place he was looking for, I told him my situation and asked if he could help with gas money. He gave me $5.00 and I was happier than ever. But reflecting back on my situation, I truly believe he was an angel.

After I finally made it home, I was sitting on the couch thinking about what I could do to bring in more income to help take care of my bills and my daughter. A thought came to my mind, "Why don't you throw a party, invite strippers and charge money at the door?" I remember back in the day, my mother would tell me how people would throw rent parties when people couldn't pay their rent. It was a clever idea–I thought.

I decided to go online and put an ad on Craigslist for dancers. I knew a few guys who I invited and I told them to tell their friends. See, on the south side of Atlanta in Henry County and nearby counties, there wasn't much to do. I started charging $10 to get in and I let the dancers keep all of their tips. Pretty soon everyone on the south side knew Courtney had the girls and from there, as we say these days, it went viral. Once the word spread that I was throwing parties, I started traveling and doing parties for birthdays, holidays, bachelor parties and other events. Now, I was too shy to dance, but I was able to orchestrate the parties. I would throw parties every weekend to make enough money to help pay my bills and other expenses and it helped out a lot.

I've always been the person to help others and the girls that would dance for me depended on me. I remember I would get phone calls from the dancers asking if I'm throwing a party. Once I started getting money, it was no longer about me. I felt that these dancers needed me so I continued to throw parties to help them out. Some of them also had kids, but were not getting help from their children's fathers.

I called the group, Lollipop Entertainment. At one point, I had 10 dancers working or ready to work with just a simple phone call from me to let them know we had another party booked. Lollipop Entertainment was the name because we would have dancers from different ethnicities; everyone likes something different. Most of the dancers and I were like family. There are still a few who I have contact with now 10 years later.

While working at the bank in the daytime and throwing parties on weekends, I kept searching for a better job opportunity. I would fill out applications all the time hoping that one day I would get a chance to just be able to work one job that would be able to supply all of my needs and finances. That one day came when I was 25 and received a phone call from Clayton County Police Department.

You never know what challenge you may face in life, so I've learned not to judge others. Who knows what career your kids or grandkids may have or what they may have to do to survive. See, at that time in my life, I was at the bottom trying to make enough money to just meet my basic needs. It seems that when you're down there is no one there to help you, but as soon as you come up, everyone wants to be around you or there for you.

Regardless, I just kept grinding, hoping and praying that one day I would get my breakthrough; hoping that I could find ONE decent job. I would pray to God every day. Little did I know that he was molding me to be who I am today.

I was being put through a test and I guess it was to help other women, maybe single moms, who are going through what I went through. I'm here to say, keep your head up and things will get better.

In the near future, I am looking to start a nonprofit organization for single moms and teen moms who I can reach and mentor through my testimony because there is a way out of the misery.

6
Clay Co.

Walking in the door from work one day, I went to check the caller ID and saw that I had a missed call from the Clayton County Police Department. I'm thinking to myself, "Why are they calling me?" I go check my messages and it was in reference to a job opportunity for a 911 dispatcher! You better be careful what you ask for, because you just might get it and boy was I happy. I felt like I can finally start making more money to support myself and my daughter without doing any parties or working two and three jobs. And, I can have more time for myself and Shimiya.

I called them back and they set me up to take a typing test. I guess that keyboarding class I took in high school was worth it. I did 10-key data entry at Wells Fargo for about six years, plus I'd been keying since I was 15. I aced the test and then they scheduled me for a second interview of which I did well. I then had to take a lie detector test. I was a bit nervous because I didn't know what type of questions they were going to ask me. My record was clean. I have never had a speeding ticket, but I was worried because I was throwing parties and didn't know how that would look even though I was doing it to provide for my family. I really wanted this job, so I ended up letting go of Lollipop Entertainment. When I explained to the girls that I wasn't going to be throwing parties anymore, some of them were hurt, but most of them understood.

I knew in order for me to progress in life, I needed to have a good paying job with benefits. I passed the lie detector test and was hired as a Clayton County 911 dispatcher. I started working there in 2011. I gave a two-week notice to Wells Fargo and was on my way to a new adventure and a new career. They started me off with $16.50 hour and they had a lot of overtime. Training took the longest because I had to get signed off of every radio they had. I also had to learn the signals and codes that were used over the radios. And, I needed to know the lingo and how to dispatch the officers.

The room would be loud and noisy, especially when there was someone running from the police. Boy, did it get loud. You would have District 1 screaming and letting the whole floor know what's going on. It was a really fun environment and it was something different. I didn't have to worry about falling asleep in there, unlike Wells Fargo, where you had to be quiet. They barely wanted you to talk so it was much easier to fall asleep.

Training, in all, took about a year and there was two weeks at an academy in Forsyth, Georgia that was required. Once trained on all radios, fireside was my favorite. We would deal with all of the medical calls, house fires and apartment fires. I would get 20 to 30 hours of overtime every week. And now, I was making about $1,000 dollars a week with overtime.

I met some really amazing people at Clayton County who taught me a lot. We would also hang out after work sometimes and socialize. I ended up getting a house in McDonough when I was 25. Life was getting much better for us. I had paid off my truck and had even bought my little brother, Brandon, his first car. I was really proud of myself and the accomplishments and transition I made. My daughter's father, Gerald, was still in the Army and was now living in Germany. He would call Shimiya and FaceTime her when he could.

While working for the police department life was great and I was making money, but I had to work so much overtime to make the money. I still wanted more. I wanted to be home with my daughter and to see her more often. I worked the 2nd shift which started at 3 PM, so I would need to be at work around 2:45. Normally, when I would leave the house, Shimiya was still at school so the only time I would see her is when I got off work around 11 PM or 3 AM, if I decided to work overtime. I was happy with my finances, but I wasn't happy because I was always working.

I had to come up with an alternative. I was thinking of work from home jobs that I could do and hopefully transition from the police department to working from home and having it all. By the way, there were several people who were working from home and making a great living. I just had to figure it out.

I started going on YouTube, believe it or not, and researching work from home jobs and I found two companies that I might be interested in–Arise and Live-Ops. I did my research on the companies and next thing I know, something tragic happens. My daughter's father passed away in Germany.

7
An Unexpected Tragedy

When I heard the news, it was surreal. I couldn't believe what I was hearing from the other end of the phone.

One night while driving home, I decided to stop and get some gas since I was running low on fuel. While pumping the gas, I received a phone call from Nate, Shimiya's uncle and her father's brother. He said, "Courtney, I got to tell you something.

I said, "Ok. Go ahead. What is it?

He then proceeds to tell me that Gerald's dead. I looked at the phone because I couldn't believe what I was hearing from the other end.

I responded, "Nate, stop playing."

He said, "No, Courtney. I'm serious."

Shimiya was over her grandmother's house when it happened and they both had just finished talking on the phone with him just a few hours before. I asked Nate what happened while at the same time my heart started beating fast and my hands started sweating. Nate wasn't too sure, but he did say that Gerald was on a treadmill and he passed out. As Nate was talking, tears started flowing down my face. I thought, "Is this real? My high school love is gone forever." I had to be dreaming.

Ever since I've known Gerald, he always worked out. He was in weight lifting when I met him in when I was in my P.E. class in high school. He loved working out. He joined the military at 17 and would run outside 4-5 miles every day. He was in perfect shape and good health. It was very hard to understand how he could come home and pass out on a treadmill. They eventually said the cause of death was a heart attack. At 28 years old! He was still very young. The military ended up flying his body back to Georgia from Germany where we were able to see him and have his funeral.

My daughter is the type of person who tries to hold everything in just like her mom. I was that same girl. Before the funeral, she wrote her father a letter and placed it inside his casket. The tears just started flowing down her face. Seeing her cry made me hurt on the inside even more because now my daughter doesn't have a father. It was really hard to deal with especially after everything was over and my daughter returned to school. I would get phone calls every day from the school saying Shimiya won't eat, or she's not doing her work. They basically described her as being a zombie! It was hard to digest. I would have to go to the school every day it seemed and sometimes right before having to go to work at the police department. Now, I knew I had to do something and something fast. I couldn't stand seeing my daughter hurting and with all the hours I was working at the police department, something had to give. I needed to be home with her to help her heal, but I still had bills. What was I supposed to do? I decided that I must step out on faith and let Jesus take the wheel. I went harder with Live-Ops and making phone calls so I could build up enough revenue to work at home as a call center agent. I would take Pizza Hut orders, Beachbody and so much more. I would normally make the orders before to going into work, so I could see if it would be feasible for me to leave my good paying job with benefits at the police department. I had been dreaming about that job for all those years of working two and three jobs.

Corey would call from prison; he was getting out soon. He would revert our conversations back to trucking because trucking was always his dream. He said, "Courtney, I've told you before, why don't you broker freight. You can work from home on the computer that you love. Broker a few loads and you're done for the day. You have the rest of the day to yourself to do whatever you want and you can be home with Shimiya."

All of the other times, I would turn his idea down. Now, I had a reason to think about it. Now, I had a motive. Now, I knew that I needed a change. I told him that when he got out that I would give it a try. I felt that I've tried everything else. Why not give it a shot? Who knows where it will take me?

I will say that was the best thing that I could have ever done. Corey served 12 years in federal prison and when he got out he was ready to get to work. He had always been a hard worker and provider; he had the mentality that he had to make it work for him and his five kids. He started teaching me everything about freight brokering, what a factoring company was, how the factoring companies worked. He taught me everything about brokering and I never attended a freight brokering school. In my book about how to be a freight broker agent, I talk briefly about how we started a brokerage. It was extremely hard and we had to close it. At the time when we started the brokerage, I would spend hours every week calling shippers. My brother would wake me up at 5 and 6 AM every morning saying, "Let's get to work" or "Are you ready to work?" He was very militant and determined. I stepped out on faith and left the police department with only about $6,000 dollars saved. That wasn't much but I was like, "God, I'm going to listen to you and let you be my provider. I know I can make it."

Making phone calls to shipper day in and day out wasn't going anywhere. I wanted to give up big time because I was calling all of these shippers, not even moving one load. And, on top of that, I wasn't making any money and we had monthly bills coming in from the brokerage. What in the world did my brother get me into? That's why I state on my videos that it's very important to try to make 200 phone calls a day if you can because brokering isn't easy. You must be persistent. I finally got my first shipper which was a lunchmeat shipper and I moved my first load.

A few months went by, and to me, the brokerage was slow. We closed the brokerage. At that time, my brother was still in the halfway house and was limited to what he could do and I was running everything; it was too hard. We decided to put the brokerage on pause and he would open up his trucking company. The trucking company made money faster because after you pick up and deliver a load, you factor it and get paid the same day or the next day. We could make money faster with the trucking company and then invest that into brokerage to make it stronger and better.

Another thing I've learned is that life is short. You have to love people while they are here. Never go to bed with anger in your heart and forgive others while they are here. You never know what life is going to bring or throw at you. Have faith. See, I never knew what God was preparing me for when I left the police department and went to seek work from home opportunities. Neither did I know that my career would also be in trucking after my brother had tried for years to get me started in trucking.

Life is like a box of chocolate just like Forest Gump said in his movie. Take care of yourself while you can and work on careers that make you happy and provide a steady income. It's also very important to make sure you have life insurance for you and your -family members. There are a lot of truckers who have no insurance and they are the bread winners in their family.

8
Bumble Bee

You might be asking how I started my company, Bumble Bee. Well, it's simple. I came up with the name from the car that I purchased about a year prior. I have a yellow and black Dodge Charger Daytona edition which reminds me of a transformer vehicle. I called my car the Bumble Bee well before ever thinking about starting this company. When I found out that I was pregnant with my second child, I started thinking of other work from home ideas. I had left the police department and was doing call center work at home jobs. This was before I really got deep into the trucking industry. I drove for Uber when the company first started here in Atlanta. The problem was that I was 6 months pregnant and if I sat for long periods of time, my legs would swell. So I came up with other ideas in which I could be closer to my home and not have to drive through downtown Atlanta traffic. I lived about 30 miles from downtown Atlanta in McDonough, which is located in Henry County. Uber wasn't in McDonough yet, only in downtown Atlanta.

I then came up with the idea that I would start a food delivery business using my car, the Bumble Bee. I named the company Bumble Bee To Go. I started planning months before launching and it really worked well. I would gather menus from all the local restaurants to gather pricing information. I had a website developer who created websites for food delivery to create my site and all I had to do was input the data. I had all the menus on the site as well as my merchant account setup. I thought this was great because I was able to work from home with a newborn baby and pick up and deliver food to people in my area. I waited until after I had my son, and until he was around five months old before I started delivering the food. I also incorporated grocery delivery with the food delivery. I used Facebook ads to generate sales and once it started taking off, I would have a few orders a day. I was proud of my success, but I didn't have any help. I was doing everything as far as dispatching myself, picking up and delivering the orders, and most of the time I was doing this with my five-month-old son in the car.

Every time I would go to a customer's door to deliver food, he would start crying as soon as I would get out of the vehicle. I would deliver to people who lived in the country clubs, even celebrities. Whenever I would go inside the country club, I would say to myself, "I'm gonna live here one day." I would close my eyes and dream about living in the country club; living like a STAR. It would last for a few seconds, then back to reality it was.

Bumble Bee was going well–around five to six orders a day, but I didn't have enough orders to hire someone and after a while and as my son started to get older, I couldn't continue with delivering the food. I closed the delivery business and started to focus more on dispatching truckers. Corey had got his trucking company up and running, which really is our company because everything was in my name and he had me running the whole company. I thank him for it because with that experience, I learned how to find the best paying loads. It allowed me to grow as an individual and my company to grow as well. Since I was already incorporated, I wasn't going to change the name of my company, so I kept the name Bumble Bee and just did more of the dispatching trucks from home.

First step, I needed clientele. I needed trucks to dispatch so I went to my favorite website, Craigslist. Remember, it was Craigslist that helped me find the strippers for the parties. Now, I was using Craigslist to help me find the truckers. I managed their company for them.

Craigslist is my site and it has played a major part in my business as far as networking with others. I put a truck dispatch ad on Craigslist and on the first day, I received a lot of responses. I remember lying across my daughter's bed and all of a sudden, my cell phone started going off. People were calling to get more information about getting their trucks dispatched and receiving freight. I couldn't believe it! I started right away with about three to four clients that I was dispatching. Four clients would generate roughly $1800- $2000 a week before I dropped our dispatching rates. I mean seriously, who makes $2000 a week working from home dispatching trucks for only about 20 hours a week? My overhead was very low; I only needed a computer, phone, the Internet and access to load boards. To me, it was the best thing ever and I loved every moment of it. Since giving birth to my son in 2014, it has allowed me to stay home with him without having to put him in daycare. I was able to pay my bills and have extra money to do what I want. After a few months, I started thinking of ways I could expand my company so I started providing services to truckers that they could use. Anything I knew how to do, I would market to the trucking community thereby creating a company that was a one-stop-shop. If you needed an authority, we did it, including permits and training. My vision was to become like the "Walmart" of the logistics industy. Bumble Bee Dispatch became a DBA of Bumble Bee To Go and it grew from there.

While dispatching owner-operators with their own authority, there were a few who didn't have trailers and were considered to be "power only" which means they have the tractor only and no trailer. You can find power only loads, but it's much better if you have a trailer. That is where our trailer division came into play. We started buying trailers and renting them out to the truckers. As you can see, in just a few short years, I was able to expand my company and make over six figures a year; mainly working from home and with low expenses.

In December of 2016, we expanded even more by starting our first YouTube Channel. YouTube was one of the best things we could have ever done because it allowed us to meet and work with amazing people all over the USA.

9
The Trucking Business

The trucking business is a hustle and it can change your life for the better, if you run and manage it correctly. The same with being a stripper. There are a lot of strippers that are college students and they actually dance in order to pay for their college expenses and graduate. Not everyone comes from wealth or a family who can help them with college expenses, so that is where the grinding comes into play. Trucking is a grind because these drivers are doing their best to get a load and get it delivered, pick up another load and keep making more money.

I will say that transportation is one industry that won't go out of business. As you look at the world today, everything that we use as consumers has to be transported to us. When you wake up in the morning and brush your teeth, where did the toothpaste come from? Maybe, Walmart. Well, how did it get there? It got there from a truck. Have you ever been to a store looking for something and you couldn't find it? You may ask a store clerk to help you find the product you're looking for and the product isn't on the shelf. And then the clerk tells you that their trucks haven't come in yet. From the gas you put in your vehicle to get to and from work to the actual vehicle you drive–both had to be transported in some way. Look at the company, UBER. They transporting people everywhere, but it's still transportation and they are doing very well.

If you want to get started into trucking, I'm here to help you and guide you. When, I first got started, there weren't a lot of people you could go to for additional help. I'm grateful because I had my brother who had over 20 years of experience in the business. Trucking is what you make it. But, once you start making money what will you do with it? Are you going to be a spender and waste it, or will you start investing your money and making it work for you. The only way to financial freedom is to obtain passive income. Passive income will allow you to live your dreams and then some. We all have a purpose in life. When you learn, teach others and if you have it, give to someone else who may be in need.

Some people think you need to have a commercial driver's license (CDL) to start a trucking business. That's not true. We set up new authorities every day. Some people have authorities and others do not, but their driver must have a CDL to operate the vehicle.

Most trucking companies will average $5,000 - $7,000 a week for a semi-truck, depending on the trailer you use and how many miles you drive. These are gross numbers so you would need to deduct your expenses to determine the net profit. Let's say you are making $20K a month from a trucking company. Do you believe that would open doors for you? Of course it would and you can take off and grow from there. Once you grow, you can help others achieve the same level of success.

Stripping and Trucking, the same grind, but different hustle. Both fields are grinding every day and are focused on accomplishing a goal. For some, it may be just to get by, pay their rent or put food on the table. Whatever the reason, they are doing what they have to do to make it. Never judge someone's occupation because you never know what you may have to do, especially if things go left and you lose your job. You never know what your kids or grandkids have to do if you're not creating a form of generational wealth now. Start planning now for your kids and grandkids so they can have an advantage when growing up. If you look at the life of Truett Cathy, founder of Chick-fil-A, he created generational wealth for his family so even though he's passed away, his corporation still exist and is doing very well. His family, for years to come, will have a foundation that will keep growing. You can do the same with trucking, look at JB Hunt, Swift, Coyotee and others. They started small and grew larger and larger over time.

You may ask, why I'm so passionate about trucking. Well, for me, trucking changed my life. It allowed me to live the life I want. I can travel whenever I'm ready and I don't have to ask for paid time off (PTO). I have flexibility. I decide what I want to do every morning when I wake up. Trucking has allowed me to invest. More importantly, it allowed me to help others who cross my path whether through

Facebook, YouTube or other sources. I've changed so many people lives and all through the message of trucking.

Trucking has its pros and cons, especially when it's time to get service done on your trucks. With proper business management you could potentially make six, seven figures or more in this field. Growing up, I never expected that I would be in the trucking industry, but again, it's the best thing I could have ever done.

10
Reflection and Vision

Looking back over the last 10 years of my life, from 22 years old to now 32 years old, I feel as if I've accomplished a lot and have grown as a woman. I'm much more mature and I don't make rash decisions I like to think and analyze things before making decisions.

Life will take you through the storm and then some, but it will mold you into a better person. Having a daughter at the age of 17 allowed me to mature and become more independent. When I started managing strippers, it was a business, however, everyone involved benefited. We became like family and had a great time. Each company I worked for would all hire me back. It's crazy because when I left the police department and stepped out on faith, I didn't give a notice and they actually called me back to work for them because of my work ethics. See people will notice your character and it could be years later before you see them again, but they won't forget you or what you did. If you are working, set personal goals and be the best employee. Go to work on time, dress appropriately and be ready for the day that lies ahead. You are preparing yourself to be a boss, so once you start running your own company you will display those same traits.

For some reason, when you become successful you may lose friends, and even family members. Not everyone will be happy for you and I've learned that the hard way. However, you will have more people that want to be around you because of your success and you have to learn how to weed out the bad seeds and surround yourself with like minded people. Choose to surround yourself with people who have similar interests. I had my brother to teach me the game, but I didn't have anyone I could go to financially. Once I improved my credit score after filing bankruptcy at the age of 21, I was able to get loans. Although it was years after filing, it was Farms Bureau Bank who gave me my first loan to buy equipment for my business and I've been winning ever since.

Over the next 10 years, there are a few ventures that I want to establish. Since I was a teen mom, I will start a nonprofit organization for young teens and single mothers to help them get on track. I want to have a pregnancy resource center where girls can come and get help, talk to counselors, and find resources to meet their needs. For the single mothers, I want to be able to create a community where we all can come together and help develop each other. They say it takes a village to raise a child and I do believe that.

I want to take the strippers out of the clubs and help them become business owners by finding out what their goals are, teaching them how to reach their goals and how to invest their money.

As far as trucking, we are already helping hundreds of people turn their lives around by starting a trucking career through Bumble Bee Dispatch. We also want to help the owner-operators grow their trucking companies and we do that through phone or in-person consultations. Our truckers social club will be in full effect in 2019. Getting the chance to be able to sit on Oprah's couch or speak with Tyler Perry about a few shows in regards to trucking would be awesome, too. Now before I go, you guys have homework to do. Please subscribe to us on YouTube @ Bumble Bee Dispatch, like us on FB, and add us on IG. Check out our contact information on the next page.

Again, I want to thank you for taking the time out to purchase my book and also read it. I'm not a seasoned author yet but maybe one day I will be. I hope you enjoyed it and if you did please leave a review and tell others about it. Stay connected so you can see what's next for Courtney Petty, and Bumble Bee!

Contact / Booking/ Get Involved

Hey Guys! Thanks for purchasing and reading my book; it means a lot to me. Most of my books are short because I like to get straight to the point and I'm not a seasoned writer yet, (lol). Again, if you feel this book will help someone you know please tell them about it.

Please feel free to connect with me in the following ways:

1. Like my FB page www.facebook.com/bumblebeedispatch to receive our latest information
2. IG cpetty85 or Bumble Bee Disp
3. Website www.bumblebeedispatch.com
4. YouTube @ Bumble Bee Dispatch
5. Email Info@bumblebeedispatch.com

Booking

If you're interested in booking me for speaking, book signing, or any other event, please send me an email with your request. We will also be hosting book signings soon, so pay attention to our Facebook and other social media outlets for updates.

Get Involved

We need volunteers for several upcoming events. Please email us for more information.

www.ingramcontent.com/pod-product-compliance
Lightning Source LLC
LaVergne TN
LVHW041635070426
835507LV00008B/633